C000220062

WHAT AM I
DOING HERE?

A beginner's guide to church

HILARY BRAND

Cartoons by
DAVE WALKER

CHURCH HOUSE
PUBLISHING

Church House Publishing
Church House
Great Smith Street
London SW1P 3AZ

Tel: 020 7898 1451
Fax: 020 7898 1449

ISBN 978 0 7151 4161 8

Published 2008 by Church House Publishing

The opinions expressed in this book are those of the
author and do not necessarily reflect the official policy
of the General Synod or The Archbishops' Council of the
Church of England.

The Scripture quotations contained herein are from the
New Revised Standard Version of the Bible, Anglicized
Edition, copyright © 1989, 1995 by the Division of
Christian Education of the National Council of the
Churches of Christ in the United States of America, and
are used by permission. All rights reserved.

Printed in England by The Cromwell Press,
Trowbridge, Wiltshire

Contents

Foreword

I will never forget the first time I went into a pub and felt utterly embarrassed. I didn't know the rules: where to sit, how to order, where to order or what to order. Everybody else seemed to know exactly what to do – they looked comfortable and I felt stupid.

Some people can feel like that when they first come to a church. The 'insiders' know what goes on and why, but assume that everybody else does too. This can make going to church a lonely and bewildering experience for people who are not familiar with what we do and why we do it.

Written from the perspective of an ordinary 'person in the pew', this book is a wonderfully direct, simple and informative guide to what goes on in church and takes us on the brief journey we make when we worship together. It is realistic and funny and debunks some of the myths about church – for example, that only 'self-righteous' people go to church. Church is for all people – the ragbag of saints and sinners that we are – and Hilary Brand's simple clarity and Dave Walker's cartoons should make it a more welcoming place, particularly for those who don't go to church but might like to.

The Rt Revd Nick Baines
Bishop of Croydon

Preface

This introduction to church and the things we do there on a Sunday morning is designed primarily for newcomers. However, it might be just as useful for those returning from a long absence, or those who've been around a long time, but never really figured what it's all about.

It comes from a Church of England publisher, so, as you might expect, it focuses on C of E style worship. And from the many variants of that, it narrows down on what is probably the most common – the Holy Communion service in the more contemporary form from *Common Worship*.[1]

It doesn't go through it in fine detail, rather it picks out those elements that are most important. And, therefore, even though it does home in on one particular service from one particular denomination, what it says about the meaning of church can be applied to a much wider spectrum.

This book wasn't written from the point of view of the person at the front with a long frock on. It was written by an ordinary pew-sitting member of the congregation – one who over the years has spent time worshipping in different denominations and different styles of church. It comes from someone who sometimes loves church and sometimes hates it, but nevertheless believes it offers something incredibly important that can't be found anywhere else!

A prayer at the start of worship

Lord our God, you know who we are: People with good and bad consciences; satisfied and dissatisfied, sure and unsure people; Christians out of conviction and Christians out of habit; believers, half-believers and unbelievers.

You know where we come from: from our circle of relatives, friends and acquaintances, or from great loneliness; from lives of quiet leisure, or from all manner of embarrassment and distress; from ordered, tense or destroyed family relationships; from the inner circle or from the fringes of the Christian community.

But now we all stand before you: in all our inequality equal in this, that we are all in the wrong before you and among each other; that we all must die some day; that we all would be lost without your grace; but also in that your grace is promised to and turned toward all of us through your beloved Son, our Lord, Jesus Christ.

We are here together in order to praise you by allowing you to speak to us. We ask that this might happen in this hour, in the name of your Son, our Lord, Amen.

Karl Barth, Swiss theologian[1]

CHAPTER

What are you doing here?

THE NEED TO MEET WITH YOUR MAKER

'You made us for yourself, 0 Lord, and our hearts are restless until they find their rest in you.'

Augustine, fifth-century North African Bishop[1]

This little book is designed to help you understand church.

Not the ceremonial of it. It is not about why everyone stands up at certain points or why there are white cloths and robes on one occasion and red on others. Nor will it unpack all the jargon. It might be handy to know what a *thurible* is or what a *lectionary* does, but they're not really that vital (although, if you do really want to know, see the Glossary at the back of the book).

Nor is it all about what Christians believe. There is much that you will need to know if you want to get a full overview of Christian teaching – why Jesus' death came to be seen as a sacrifice for all humankind; what it means when people talk about God as three in one; why Christians believe that Christ will come again – but there are plenty of other books out there that will tell you that (there are some recommendations on p. 71).

Of course, some of those things will be touched on here, but in essence this book is about something different. It is about how church services, as you go through them step by step, deal with some of the deepest things about what it means to be human. Perhaps the old name for an act of public worship: 'Divine service' can help us here. Because, when used well, what is happening can be just that:

- something to make you more 'roadworthy' for life's journey;
- a regular overhaul of your humanity from the one who made you.

What on earth brought you here?

So the first question is – what are you doing here? What made you show up at church in the first place? It's a pretty safe bet there were mixed motives involved, and that they may have included:

- I was made to go as a kid and I've never quite given up the habit.
- I fancy that girl in the choir/the youth group leader/the curate.
- Someone asked me and I didn't like to say no.
- I'm trying to please my mum/my wife/my boyfriend.
- I want my child to get a good moral education.
- I want to become part of the local community.
- I'm curious.
- I'm lonely.
- I'm bored.

REASONS FOR TRYING CHURCH

IT'S GOOD FOR
THE CHILDREN

SHE ASKED ME
TO COME ALONG

I ADMIRE THE
ARCHITECTURE

I FANCY HER

I'D LIKE TO GET
INVOLVED IN THE
COMMUNITY

I NEEDED SOMEWHERE
TO SHELTER FROM
THE RAIN

And that's the great thing about church. It's made up of other mixed-up people just like you. Mixed motives, ambivalent feelings – they're here in abundance.

You'd also probably find, if you really probe, quite a jumble of beliefs. Those up the front might appear to have it all sewn up, but chances are that many of the rest aren't quite so certain. And that's fine too. Not that beliefs don't matter, but church is not just for those who have them all sorted. Church is also for those who are searching.

What in heaven's name are you looking for?

Because, odds are that, alongside those surface motives for turning up at church, somewhere underneath – maybe quite close to the surface, maybe deep, deep down – something else is driving you.

You may not know what you're looking for. You may not be entirely convinced that you'll find it here. You may call it 'meaning' or 'purpose' or 'peace' or just something 'other'. You may or may not call it God.

Christianity (along with most other religions) claims that this need for God is at the heart of all human yearning. It's a logical claim. If you are not an accident of nature but actually designed and formed, then wouldn't you have an inbuilt deep yearning, like a child separated from birth parents, to know the one who made you?

Since you *were* designed in a way that makes you able to think and feel and form relationships, then wouldn't it make sense that you were designed for a relationship with that One who made you?

And, isn't it reasonable that the One who went to such trouble in making you uniquely *you* might actually want to help you become who you were designed to be?

This then at its absolute heart is what church is intended to be – a way of putting us in touch with our designer.

Jesus promised his followers 'life in all its fullness' (John 10.10, *Good News Bible*).[2] Church is a way of getting in touch with that life force.

What a grand statement.

But let's be honest. Church isn't always an uplifting experience. So let's deal with that right at the start.

What should you expect to get out of it?

It's sometimes said to those who come to church and don't find what they're looking for:

> *If you come away from church complaining that you've got nothing out of it, then you weren't there for the right reason.*

It's a statement that carries a lot of truth, but also some huge and complicated contradictions. So it needs a bit of careful unpacking.

Church (bringing together speech, music, movement and visual symbolism) is very much like a piece of theatre. And ideally it should do what theatre does best – send you out with a greater delight in the world and a greater understanding of it.

Church must be to some extent a performance. And if the quote above is used as an excuse for slipshod performance, then it's fair enough to question it. (Then again, it needs to be remembered that church is a performance done weekly in every town and village in the land. Sometimes it will be West End standard, but very often it will necessarily be at 'am-dram' level.)

So here's the first contradiction: church may be a performance, but it's not entertainment! Church is interactive and participatory and – here's the great genius of a written order of service – even when performed badly, it still provides a process that, if entered into, can transform you and send you away renewed.

Who is it about?

There's a much bigger contradiction at work here though. Some would say that you shouldn't come to church to get anything out of it at all. They'd say that:

Church is not about you, it's about God!

And there's truth there too. Because church is not just a 'divine service', but a divine service of *worship*. It is about coming as a humble subject to stand before an awesome, all-powerful and all-knowing monarch.

So then, you've been unhelpfully faced right at the start of this book with two contradictory statements:

- ■ Coming to church can help you become a better person, the one God wanted you to be.
- ■ If you come to church just for what you hope to get out of it, you're likely to get nothing out of it at all.

It's not a contradiction though. It's a paradox. And just in case you're not familiar with that idea, then an explanation might be helpful, because this book contains several. Indeed, Christianity itself is full of them, especially the teaching of Jesus. For example, 'All who humble themselves will be exalted' (Matthew 23.12); 'Those who lose their life for my sake will find it' (Matthew 10.39).

A paradox is when there are two opposing statements that you'd imagine couldn't both be true. Yet the deepest truth lies exactly there, by holding these two opposites in tension. It's not *either/or*, it's *both/and*. It's the sort of truth that can't be grasped by complicated mental gymnastics. It can only really be understood by trust, by taking a leap into the unknown.

And that is what church invites you to do.

2

Wonder and wow factor

THE NEED FOR CELEBRATING AND COUNTING BLESSINGS

For what has been – thanks! For what shall be – yes!

Dag Hammarskjold, Swedish statesman[1]

You've found yourself taking part in an activity called *worship*. You may find the word used even more specifically, to mean just the singing bit. And indeed singing is worship. But worship is not just singing. Worship in its truest sense is an expression of:

- reverence, respect
- adoration, awe
- paying homage to
- giving worth to.

In other words, giving God the honour and love he* deserves.

There's a bit of a problem here – often compounded by miscommunication that some churches do by accident and others, it

*I've used the male pronoun for simplicity's sake, but please be aware that God is neither male nor female. Another paradox – God is both.

seems, by design. That is to tell you that it's God who's *demanding* this worship. At the more contemporary end of the hymn spectrum are rather a lot of songs that seem to bolster this perception. What sort of God needs you to keep telling him how great he is, over and over again? Does he really need you to flatter him and butter him up? Insecure or what?

But this is a misleading view of worship. It isn't about telling God how great he is. It's about reminding yourself. Singing is intended to be that reminder, and often it is. But what if the words express things you just aren't feeling? What if God seems no more than an abstract concept, invisible and distant? There are times when, before you can express a sense of worship, you need to generate it first. Here are a few ways in:

Finding the creator through the creation

Worship begins with a shift in perspective. It's about realizing how small we are and how big God is. It's about ceasing just for a while to see ourselves as the centre of the universe. Of course, church isn't the only place where this mental shift can be made, and maybe not always the best. Some people may get a much better sense of it out walking on the hills, peering at the iridescent intricacy of a dragonfly, listening to a soaring orchestra, or watching the crash of the waves. That could, of course, be an argument for spending Sunday mornings outside church. It's not how 'worship' is being used here, since there are other times to enjoy God's creation and other reasons to come to church. But giving ourselves time to stop and drink in the 'wow factor' of life is an essential element of worship. If we have done that throughout the week, if only for the odd moment, then church gives a chance to stop, recall and reflect on those glimpses, to find the transcendent among the ordinary.

Flexing your gratitude muscles

It's official. Gratitude is good for you. Several psychological research projects point to the same conclusion:

> *Individuals who regularly experience and express gratitude are physically healthier, more optimistic about the future, and feel better about their lives than those who do not. Individuals who experience gratitude are more alert, enthusiastic and energetic than those who do not, and they are more likely to achieve personal goals.*[2]

And, says the psychologist from whom that quote comes:

> *Experiencing and expressing gratitude actually get easier with practice.*[3]

So church is a great place for a regular workout in thanksgiving – looking back and celebrating the many good things that have come into the week. There's no need to pretend that all is hunky-dory if it is not. But it's guaranteed: even in the darkest days, if you look for them, some amazing glimmers of goodness will shine out.

Feeling yourself loved

Apologies for cramming this small book with so many paradoxes, but here's another one. Worship is not only about realizing how small you are and how big God is, it's also about comprehending that, however insignificant you might feel yourself to be, in God's eyes you are very, very important.

When did you last ponder the astonishing fact of your own uniqueness? There is nowhere, never has been and never will be,

HYMN SINGING

anyone quite like you. You undoubtedly wish you had been made in some way different – smaller thighs, straighter nose, a better way with quick repartee – but what if God loves you just as you are, is hugely proud of you, absolutely delights to see you coming along the road, is thrilled to bits when you talk to him, be it 'Please', 'Thank you', 'How?' or 'Why?'. What if God is, in fact, the kind of heavenly father Jesus said he was?

Of course, we bring to church with us all sorts of baggage, which may make the use of the male term 'father' difficult. Some of it may be a general dislike of the prominence of the male gender – in which case it's worth remembering that the Bible also refers to God as a mother (see Isaiah 49.15-16 and 66.13) and simply substituting the equally valid word 'parent' in your own mind. But, more seriously, some of it may be bad experiences of being parented, especially by a father. In the light of that, divine love may be something that is very hard to *feel*. But in the same way that gratitude can be worked on, so can knowing yourself loved. Many of the hymns or songs encountered in church will reflect this theme: 'Great is thy faithfulness', 'Amazing grace', 'My song is love unknown', 'Such love, pure as the whitest snow'. Remember as you sing them that they are not just wishful-thinking, cosy sentiments from Victorian poets or guitar-wielding Christian pop stars. Most of the words you find in these songs are rooted deep in the Bible, the New Testament in particular. This deep committed love is the theme song of the whole book.

The circular nature of this whole paradox (the 'both/and', rather than 'either/or' nature of spiritual truths) is, of course, that it's only when you truly know yourself loved that you are able to stop worrying about your own importance. It's then that you're able to stop striving for your place in the world, stop struggling to prove yourself, and become fully able to look beyond yourself to your world and your neighbour.

Filling your lungs

An aside worth noting: singing is good for you. Not only does it improve your psychological well-being, releasing 'feel-good' hormones called endorphins and generating a sense of togetherness; done with a certain amount of vigour, it also boosts lung capacity, improves posture, exercises your face muscles, increases oxygenation in the bloodstream and makes you mentally more alert.

As human attributes go, song hardly seems vital, just an optional extra, one of God's excessive flourishes on the creation cake. After all, many people never sing at all apart from in the shower. But what a waste for creatures made with an inbuilt sense of wonder, with a capacity for joy and celebration, never to express it in this remarkable way. If we're creatures made to reach out to our creator, then maybe praising in song is an essential way to do it.

And what a waste to sing only alone. There's something quite remarkable about many voices raised in song together – an activity that all ages can participate in. If, as a parent, you've brought your children to church (and more of this in Chapter 7, p. 45) then singing is a great activity for parents and children to share together.

(Some people may say they can't sing – although they probably mean they can't sing *in tune*. How much this matters is a moot point. If a magnificent choral performance is the object of the exercise then perhaps full volume should be reserved for the shower. But if the purpose is to glorify God, then it's arguable that he delights in our gusto and lack of inhibition however tuneless!)

Finding what works

Even so, not everyone finds singing (or reading aloud) helpful, so give yourself permission to be silent if that is what works for you. It may be helpful to note a phrase from a song or spoken response that is meaningful and use it as a focus for your thoughts.

It's important to remember too that there are many other ways of worshipping God and many things that can be said without words. Churches vary in their expectations of how to use body language. In some, crossing yourself and bowing before the altar are the norm (see the Glossary for more definition). In others, hands may be raised in song or prayer, there may be clapping or even the rare bit of dance! In most churches it's customary to stand for the Gospel reading, honouring the words and actions of Jesus, and for the Creed as the central heart of Christian belief. When it comes to times of prayer, some congregations stand, others kneel or sit, but most give the option and kneelers are usually available. All these are valuable ways of expressing respect and worship to God. Even if you find yourself in the most physically inhibited church in Christendom, you are actually free to use any of these means of worship (preferably without ostentation!) if you wish.

Besides all these more obvious movements in worship, it's good sometimes simply to be aware of your body, to focus for a moment on your posture as a way of stilling yourself before God. Sit straight with feet flat on the floor. De-hunch your shoulders, lift your head. Hold your hands palm upwards on your lap, as a sign of your need and willingness to receive. Become aware of your breathing. You can use even that as a sort of prayer – breathing out all that has been bad and negative in your week and breathing in God's goodness and peace in exchange.

The key in all this, perhaps, is to see yourself not just as a passive observer but as an active participant. Find what works for you – and do it.

3

Admitting and acknowledging

THE NEED FOR ACCOUNTING
PROCEDURES AND A CLEAN SLATE

*Growth begins when we start to accept our own
weakness.*

Jean Vanier, Founder of L'Arche communities[1]

There are plenty of people who'll tell you church is all about making
you feel guilty. And when you read words like these from the General
Confession in the old *Book of Common Prayer*, it somewhat reinforces
that perception:

> *We acknowledge and bewail our manifold sins
> and wickedness ... provoking most justly thy
> wrath and indignation against us.*

Bewailing doesn't seem to be a common C of E tendency, but
should it be what 'confession' is all about? Does God want us to feel
bad about ourselves? Does the church exist just to put the 'fear of
God' in us?

Guilt and grovelling

Certainly there have been times in history when 'hellfire and damnation' preachers were all the rage, and when church as an establishment institution was quite handy in putting the peasants in their place.

But no, that is not what the Prayer of Confession, an essential component of most worship services, is for. It is not intended to make us feel any worse about ourselves than we may already do.

Let's face it, many of us do already feel bad about ourselves. We know all too well our failures: our unkind thoughts, our secret vices, our bursts of temper, grumpiness, greediness, bitchiness, sloth. And most of us have highly developed coping mechanisms: sophisticated diversion tactics, smart excuses, subtle ways of passing the blame. But all the same our weaknesses do have a nasty habit of coming back to haunt us. Our tactics may slacken or soften our burden of guilt but they rarely remove it.

The purpose of confession is not to induce guilt and shame but to relieve and remove it.

It isn't for us to tell God what we've done wrong because, if God is God, then clearly he knows all about us anyway. And while that's a pretty scary concept, it can also be an immensely liberating one.

Fully known, fully loved

Marriage, friendship, partnership – most of us long to be known intimately by another. But often such closeness only reveals the distance that still remains, however long and close the relationship. You may discover that you don't want to be known. There are some things we fear revealing even to those who love us most.

But in coming before God you are coming before someone who knows you fully and still accepts you with an unrelenting, un-put-off-able love. You can't shock God. He's seen it all before.

Spotlight on 'sin'

It seems necessary here to examine briefly a word much abused and confused in the world at large, but unavoidable in a church context – 'sin'. If you find it in a newspaper headline it will undoubtedly involve sex. But although sex may involve sin – because sex beyond boundaries of commitment inevitably brings about deception, desertion, exploitation and all manner of human hurts – sin is not just about sex.

Sin, by a classic Christian definition, is: that which brings about separation from God. And very often it's not the spectacular evils that do this best: murder or bullying or fraud; but the surprisingly small ones: snide put-downs, self-absorbed insensitivity, selfish consumption. It's the things that separate us from our fellow humans that most often separate us from God.

And it's often far more to do with what we *don't* do, than with what we *do*.

The Prayer of Confession talks of sinning:

> *through negligence, through weakness, through*
> *our own deliberate fault.*

Common Worship

And while it's tempting to play down the deliberateness with which we mess up our lives and the lives of others, it is important to acknowledge that negligence – the simple absence of goodness and thoughtfulness and diligence and creativeness – does account for a vast number of the world's wrongs.

Candour and cleansing

So, in order to be free from the effect of these 'sins of commission and of omission', it's first necessary to own them.

This need not involve agonizing exercises in navel-gazing. You don't have to recall every detail. God knows. It is a simple acknowledgement: I am responsible. I messed up.

And this simple acknowledgement, this honesty and humility, is all God needs from you in order to pour in his forgiveness, to close the gap, to cleanse the toxins of shame.

Confession is an integral part of most worship services because we all need this cleansing. Look on it as a sort of colonic irrigation of the soul! Sometimes it may come as a painful purging, sometimes a gentle freshening.

Confession is vital if you want to move on and grow, because it puts you in touch with realities. For those who confess, said pioneering psychologist William James, 'shams are over and realities have begun'.[2]

Penitence and pardon

There's another unavoidable and sometimes mocked bit of religious jargon that's integral to the process of confession – 'repent'. It's not just about 'sackcloth and ashes', grovelling and cringing. Rather it is about turning around, starting again. Saying sorry is of limited value if there is not the slightest intention of change. Intention is the key word here – little point in pretending you won't mess up again! Repentance is 'sorry and . . .' not 'sorry but . . .'.

In an Anglican service of worship, the Prayer of Confession never stands alone. Always it is followed by the pronouncing of an Absolution – the 'giving' of God's mercy, pardon and deliverance. Of course, no priest has the power in themselves to wipe the slate clean. But he or she takes on an authority that Jesus gave to his disciples at the Last Supper (John 20.23) to be agents of God in passing on the forgiveness that only God can give.

But forgiveness does need to be accepted. It's quite possible to work through a catalogue of your shortcomings and never forgive yourself. That's essentially self-centred. If God has forgiven you – and the whole story of Christianity is that this forgiveness is given at great sacrificial cost – then who are you not to accept?

Take the gift, stand tall, move on. Learn to live in real holiness in the same way as Brazilian Archbishop Helder Camara:

> *Being holy means getting up immediately every time you fall, with humility and joy . . . It means being able to say, 'Yes, Lord, I have fallen a thousand times. But thanks to you, I have got up a thousand and one times.'*[3]

CHAPTER

4

The Bible – and bashing it!

THE NEED FOR WISE WORDS
AND CHALLENGING QUESTIONS

I have found in the Bible words for my inmost
thoughts, songs for my joy, utterance from my hidden
griefs and pleadings for my shame and feebleness.

Samuel Taylor Coleridge, nineteenth-century poet[1]

Someone has just come up to the lectern and read a few paragraphs
that sound obscure and a little confusing. They end with the
statement 'This is the word of the Lord.'

The Bible – 'meat and drink to the soul' or 'dry as a stick', however
you view it – is the central foundation of the Christian faith. Depending
on the style of church, reverence for it will be expressed in different
ways. It may be brought forward in solemn procession preceded by
incense; the priest may bend to kiss it. At the other end of the spectrum,
reverence may be expressed simply by the length of time allotted
to a sermon explaining it. Whatever the tradition, respect is usually
shown by standing as the words of the Gospel (the story and teaching
of Jesus) are read. Either way, this book is regarded as a precious
authority, a medium through which the voice of God can be heard.

So how can we begin to tune in?

A library of diverse literature

Perhaps the best way to begin is to look at what the Bible is not. It is not, in fact, a single, book written by one author and offering a coherent world view. It is a collection of books written by different hands over at least a thousand- year period and referring to events that span at least twice that. It encompasses a rich variety of literary styles: poetry, history, eyewitness accounts, ancient tales, anecdotes, pithy sayings, rules for society, complex theological explanations – that need to be read and understood in vastly different ways.

Because of this diversity of era, author and style, it explores truth from many different viewpoints, and charts an evolution of understanding: about meaning, about morals and about God. (It is remarkable, though, how the words of Jesus stand out, with a timelessness and authority, above the rest.)

A breath of fresh air

But, given this diversity, how are we expected to understand everything we hear as 'the word of the Lord'? Perhaps the best definition of why this collection of writings has come to be so special is found in the words of the apostle Paul to his apprentice Timothy:

> *All scripture is God-breathed.*
>
> **2 Timothy 3.16, New International Version**[2]

That means not that every word is infallible or every instruction directly relevant to the twenty-first century, but that within these writings God's Spirit can breathe. That down through the centuries and across different cultures, countless people have found there wisdom, advice, comfort and challenge for their needs.

So don't worry if sometimes you find it 'dry as a stick'. It was John Bunyan, seventeenth-century author of *The Pilgrim's Progress*, who recorded that sometimes the whole Bible seemed that way to him. He also noted, however, its richness, power and directness:

> *I have sometimes seen more in a line of the Bible*
> *than I could well tell how to stand under …*[3]

And don't worry if sometimes it makes no sense. As Mark Twain famously observed:

> *Most people are bothered by the passages of scripture*
> *which they cannot understand, but as for me, I have*
> *always noticed that the passages in scripture which*
> *trouble me most are those which I do understand.*[4]

It was George Whitfield, a famous eighteenth-century preacher, who recorded in his journal that the Bible was 'meat indeed and drink to my soul'. But it's worth noting that this happened when he began to 'read the holy scriptures upon my knees'.[5] In other words, this came not just by hearing the Bible once a week but by reading it for himself and praying over what he read.

A two-way process

The important principle is that Bible reading is an interactive process. Its God-breathed-ness did not just come through the ancient act of writing the words, it can come afresh to each individual through the act of reading or hearing them.

A few suggestions on how to get the most from the Bible readings you hear in church:

- ■ Ask God to speak to you through them.
- ■ Although it's often a powerful experience just to *hear* the words, if there's a Bible available in church, it may be helpful to look up the passages and read

them. This will help you focus on the words and may also give a sense of the wider context.

- Make a note of the passages and when you get home dust off your Bible, if you have one (see the note on p. 28), and read them for yourself. Also look at what comes before and after each passage to get a bit of background.
- Notice any particular phrases that strike you. Ask yourself why they seemed significant.
- Note anything that made you uncomfortable or that you didn't understand. Put the vicar on the spot afterwards by asking for an explanation! Alternatively, take time to ponder. The passages that raise more questions than answers can sometimes be the ones that teach you most.

A lot of hot air?

And then comes the sermon.

One of the definitions my dictionary gives for 'to preach' is: 'to give advice in an offensive, tedious or obtrusive manner'.

Hopefully the sermons you listen to are not like that.

Sermons, or homilies as they are sometimes called, can be, at best, brilliant examples of the neglected art of oration. Let's look at what they are intended to do:

- Teach: simply to explain a Bible passage or aspect of the Christian faith;
- Exhort: 'to urge strongly and earnestly';
- Inspire: to influence with emotion, or literally to 'draw in breath' – in other words to encourage you to breathe in God's Spirit.

Sermons do have limitations though.

Genuine inspiration is great. Unfortunately we've all heard motivational speakers who blow us away with uplifting words that on later analysis seem little more than hot air. That's why thinking it through afterwards is so important.

Exhortation can be vital – there are times when we all need to be told in no uncertain terms to buck our ideas up. The problem of repeated exhortations from the pulpit is that they can give the idea that you're never good enough, that there's always something else you should be doing. If this is the case, then take care to listen honestly for what God might be telling you, and feel free to jettison the rest.

A message from God

So, how to get the most from a sermon? Some of the suggestions on Bible reading also apply here and there are also a couple of more subversive ones:

- ■ Ask God to speak to you through it. It's been frequently observed that the voice of God is just as able to communicate in tin chapels as in soaring cathedrals, through naive choruses as well as through complicated cantatas, and through someone plain-spoken or inarticulate as much as through someone eloquent – and maybe even more so. God is no snob and it seems he likes to use humble instruments.

- ■ Again look out for phrases that hit you or that you find difficult or uncomfortable. The purpose of a sermon is, to use a much quoted phrase: 'to comfort the afflicted and afflict the comfortable'.[6] Which do you need more right now?

- Don't be surprised if it raises more questions than it gives answers. Maybe there simply hasn't been enough time for full explanation. Maybe, though, what you're encountering is paradox – a truth that lies in the tension between two seemingly competing ideas. Live with the questions; don't try to dodge them. Only then can they reveal their wisdom.
- Don't let the preacher get away with it. The fact that they're in a pulpit doesn't really mean they're 'six feet above contradiction'. If they use difficult jargon, make assumptions or say something you disagree with, then ask for explanations. Do it at the time if you're brave enough, though afterwards is probably better! Most preachers will welcome this. It does at least mean someone is listening.
- If it's really irretrievably boring, then tune it out, go back to the Bible passage and think it out for yourself!

Taking it further

When it comes to teaching, the ten-to-twenty-minute length of most sermons is simply not long enough to explain much properly. It's also strangely 'one of the last forms of public discourse where it is culturally forbidden to talk back'.[7] That's why finding Christian teaching in other forms: in group study, in courses such as Alpha or Emmaus, or by reading, are pretty well essential if you're seriously seeking to understand more about the Christian faith.*

Why not ask the church leaders about such groups?

*The Further reading section (p. 70) gives suggestions on what Bible translations you may find the most helpful, other resources to help you with Bible reading and some materials that explain the basics of Christian faith.

THE SERMON

DO NOT BE AFRAID TO ASK QUESTIONS WHEN IT HAS FINISHED

CHAPTER

5

Bottom line and benchmark

THE NEED FOR A BASIC BELIEF SYSTEM

The majority of people live below the level of belief or doubt.

T. S. Eliot, poet[1]

Chances are, if you are a newcomer to church, you may be a little uncertain of what you believe. So when it comes to the Creed, that part of the service when everyone recites together a statement of faith, you may feel a little unsure how to react:

- Do you speak it out, keeping your doubts as a private whisper in your head?
- Do you just mumble along?
- Do you only say the bits you really believe and stop where you don't?

There isn't, as far as I know, a right answer to this but, to help you decide, it's worth examining what the purpose of these statements is.

An ancient consensus

The most common in use (and the one you're most likely to hear Sunday by Sunday) is the Nicene Creed. It has a very long history, dating back to AD 325 when Christians from different branches of the Church met together in Nicaea in present-day Turkey to agree on a statement of what they believed. The resulting document, refined over the centuries and with just a few variations, is still used today in Roman Catholic, Anglican, Orthodox and many Protestant churches worldwide.

There's something very reassuring about this statement – it's unifying, it's solid, it's stood the test of time. It rests firmly on the Bible record and on the basics that all mainstream Christians share: that Jesus was and is the Son of God and that through his death and resurrection is offered to every individual something remarkable called 'salvation'. It offers a 'grand story' about the meaning of life, a solid ground of truth standing out above a restless sea of doubt.

A postmodern world view

The problem is that we live in what has been called a 'postmodern' culture, a sceptical society where grand stories of meaning are generally dismissed and anyone who holds on to Truth with a capital T is seen as somehow suspect.

Of course, there are reasons for this. We live in a multi-faith world. It's no longer possible to cling to one brand of religion by pretending others don't exist. We also live in a materialist and rationalist society where militant atheists such as Richard Dawkins proclaim that:

> Faith is the great cop-out, the great excuse to
> evade the need to think and evaluate evidence.
> Faith is belief in spite of, even perhaps because of,
> the lack of evidence.[2]

THE CREED

So for anyone who does want to believe but doesn't want to evade the need to think, the Creed may present something of a problem. You're being asked to affirm belief in supernatural events that happened 2,000 years ago. You may feel a little like Alice in

Wonderland, being told by the White Queen to believe 'six impossible things before breakfast'.[3]

Do you have to be fully signed up to all of this before you're allowed to be a fully fledged Christian? Do you not only have to believe in the virgin birth and the Holy Trinity, but be able to explain them too?

That might rule quite a few of us out.

And does 'believing in' mean you're so passionately convinced that you'd lay down your life rather than deny any one of these articles of faith, or does it mean that you have a basic belief in God and are prepared to go along with the details?

A point to aim for

The answer to that depends on whether you view the Creed as a bottom line or a benchmark. If it's a bottom line, then it's logical that you sign up to every one of its tenets before you call yourself Christian, but if it's a benchmark, things are a bit different. Then it stands, if you like, as a mark of doctrinal excellence – a fixed point of reference, an agreed standard, something to respect and assent to and to aspire to believing fully.

In some senses the Creed is a bottom line. Can you imagine how Christianity as a whole would fare if each denomination, each generation, each individual congregation decided to make its own statement of what it believed? It would certainly be an interesting exercise, but picture the arguments, divisiveness and confusion that would result!

But in another way – and this is the way that affects you as an individual making tentative steps towards faith – it stands as a benchmark:

- not something to mumble and privately disregard;
- not something to beat yourself up about if you're not sure;

- but something to respect and seek to understand;
- something to accept as divine revelation and the product of wise minds;
- something to aspire to believe fully.

A risky journey

It's important to remember that Jesus clearly didn't think you had to pass an exam in religious theory before you could become one of his followers. He could have spent his time expounding doctrinal mysteries but chose instead to tell simple stories that had much more to do with how to live than what to believe. He was happy to let the whole edifice of the Church rest on unlearned human foundations – wavering Peter, doubting Thomas – that some might consider just a little shaky.

The essential thing about Christian faith is not *what you believe* but *whom you trust*. It's not about a *sewn-up list of certainties* but a *daily walk of obedience*.

So when you say: 'I believe ...' you're not negating the need to think or claiming certainties you cannot prove. You're taking a risk, based on an entirely different level of evidence, one that the scientists can never measure, but which life itself simply can't do without – love, conscience, wonder, beauty, trust, and indeed pain and evil.

It will be a journey of discovery. It may be a struggle. It certainly won't be a cop-out.

6

Problems and petitions

THE NEED TO ENGAGE WITH THE WIDER WORLD AND ASK FOR HELP

Properly understood and applied, prayer is the most potent instrument of action.

Mahatma Gandhi, Indian political activist[1]

Most church services are dotted throughout with prayer. By the time you've got past the sermon, you will already have had a prayer of Preparation, of Confession and often something mysteriously known as a 'Collect', which simply means the Prayer Book's written prayer of the day. But then there comes an item generally referred to as 'Prayers', or to give it its proper title: Prayers of Intercession.

And in this case, understanding the proper title is important, because intercession, defined in the dictionary as 'the act of pleading for another', is not all that prayer is, but just one part of it. The trouble is, it's the part that we all start off with:

God bless mummy and daddy and Cedric the hamster and look after the poor people – and by the way, can I have a new bike?

So it's easy to see prayer just as asking, and all too often just as reciting a list of worthy causes, and sometimes never get beyond this understanding.

Prayer is far more than this. It has many forms and can be practised in all sorts of places – anywhere and at any time, in fact – and at its most potent has a great deal more to do with listening than talking. At its heart, prayer is simply conversation with God, so if you never converse with him alone – like any conversation, listening as well as talking – then praying in church is probably not going to mean much to you. (And that could be the subject of a whole other book.)* But with that big proviso in place, let's return to the idea of 'prayers' in church.

The whole world in our hands

Typically, Prayers of Intercession will begin with the wider world – the latest earthquake or famine or conflict – then move on to those in authority – the queen, the government, church leaders – before returning to the local community – the church roof fund, the youth work, those who are sick or troubled – and then homing in on us as individuals who, of course, need to be better people in one way or another.

The trouble is that you're not a fool. You're not really convinced that African dictators, capitalist exploitation or Cynthia's cancer will suddenly vanish in the face of our mumbled 'Amens'. You don't really believe that God is about to wipe away all pain and oppression, just because today you happened to ask.

So this sort of prayer is bound to confront you with uncomfortable questions. The issue of why a loving God allows good people to suffer is perhaps the biggest obstacle to faith that many people have.

(There *are* some answers to be grasped – to do with freedom and moral choice and what it means to be a conscious being and not an automaton – and they're inescapably logical ones if you look at the subject in depth.)*

But if you acknowledge that, for whatever reason, suffering and evil are part of the human condition and here to stay, what's the point of these prayers? Is it just to remind us of the needy world beyond our doorstep?

Well, even if that were the only reason, it might be no bad thing. Intercession brings you face to face once again with the troubles of the world – the distant ones you've seen on the news, the closer ones you've heard about on the grapevine – and makes you see them in a new light. Not through the dispassionate TV lens or the judgement of gossip, but through the eyes of a caring compassionate Father God who weeps for his foolish children and the mess they've made of his world. Seen from this perspective they claim more than your curiosity. They call out for compassion and demand that you care.

A wing and a prayer

But at this point, faced not only with your limited capacity to understand, but also with your inability to effect change, if you're not careful you could be overwhelmed by the whole enterprise. So it's here that you have a choice, either to switch off or to begin the real work of prayer.

It's curious that those who frequently engage in this sort of prayer – monks and nuns and so on – often speak of it as work. They see it not as a substitute for social action or a poor second-best. It's been called 'the most intensely social act that a human being is capable of',[2] 'the supreme weapon in the struggle in which we are called to take part'.[3]

Of course, that makes no sense if you believe that the struggle for good and evil takes place purely at a practical level. But if you

* See suggested reading on prayer or suffering (p. 72)

PRAYER

HOW IT MIGHT WORK

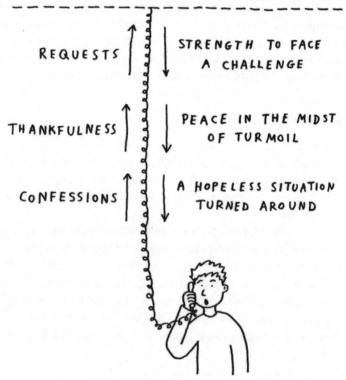

WE DO NOT
UNDERSTAND THE
BIT ABOVE THIS LINE

REQUESTS — STRENGTH TO FACE A CHALLENGE

THANKFULNESS — PEACE IN THE MIDST OF TURMOIL

CONFESSIONS — A HOPELESS SITUATION TURNED AROUND

believe there may be something beyond our four dimensions, even if you are unclear what, then it's a different matter. Even if you can't comprehend how it might work, you can appreciate that there could be a whole other dimension to this struggle going on beyond what you can see.

Scientists exploring the complexities of nature through Chaos Theory have summed up the way that tiny variants can result in vast changes with the much-quoted idea that 'when a butterfly flaps its wings in Tokyo it unleashes a tornado in Texas'.[4]

So why shouldn't that same theory work in a spiritual dimension? Why shouldn't your small longing for justice, your tiny cry for mercy, when linked with all those other 'wing flaps' of concern make the world into a better place?

Calling a spade a digging implement

It's a theory. All the same, no one as yet can explain how prayer works. Fortunately, just because you can't explain how it works, it doesn't mean you can't use it.

Catherine Bramwell-Booth, granddaughter of the founder of the Salvation Army, summing up her views at the age of 100, put it like this:

> *Prayer is part of the mystery of life . . . The man*
> *in the street used to be content to call a spade a*
> *spade. Now even he, or anyway his son knows*
> *that a spade is composed of infinitesimal particles*
> *so small that no microscope can make them*
> *visible to the human eye, that these particles are*
> *each an ordered universe of 'bodies' revolving in*
> *space . . . The atomic mystery of the spade may be*
> *a mystery too wonderful for me, but that doesn't*
> *prevent me from using it to dig with.*[5]

So if you do engage in this work of prayer, what sort of difference can you expect to make?

First, something that's important to remember: 'Prayer is request' said C. S. Lewis, 'and the essence of request is that it may or may not be granted.'[6]

Even Jesus himself prayed on the eve of his crucifixion that this ordeal might be avoided. It was not. Jesus died and through it we are offered redemption. Prayer does not always avert evil, but it may bring from it a greater good than could ever have been dreamed of.

But miracles do happen – Christians down the ages and around the world have given plenty of testimony to that. True, the sorts of miracle we might hope for – tumours shrunk, floods held back – are rare. Much more frequent is the evidence of strength to face a challenge, peace in the midst of turmoil, safety in the eye of the storm, a situation turned around when it seemed hopeless – when it comes to these sorts of miracle, there are millions of people to attest that they happen.

If you're a beginner in prayer, then the sort of big-scale intercessions you often find in church – global warming, wars, earthquakes – aren't the best place to start. That's why personal prayer, praying for your own needs and the needs of those closest to you, is especially important. Because, when you begin to see it making a difference in your own life and in the lives of those around you, then you may be able to glimpse what difference it could make in situations you may never know or see.

God cares for sparrows and flowers and little children and tax collectors and prostitutes, said Jesus (Matthew 6.26–29; 10.29–30; Matthew 19.13–15; Luke 5.27–32; Matthew 21.31; Luke 7.36–50). No one is too insignificant for his care and nothing too trivial to bring to him. So in prayer you can bring to God your tiniest concerns – yes, even Cedric the hamster – as well as the biggest issues of poverty and justice.

Part of the problem, part of the solution

Of course, at both these extremes and for everything in between, God may suggest that you yourself are the answer to your prayers. In fact, used rightly, that too is a major part of these prayers. As we pray for our world, we are also acknowledging that we might be part of the problem, and asking that instead we become part of the solution. We are asking that our wills be brought into line with God's. So as you participate in the intercessions, don't forget to listen. Make a note of any thoughts that come to you in prayer, think them through and then don't forget to act on them. You can't take on the problems of the whole world, but that tiny God-prompted prayer-inspired action might make all the difference.

Handshakes and hugs

THE NEED TO LIVE IN RIGHT RELATIONSHIP WITH OTHERS

Where there is no mutual relationship there is no human experience of God.

Chung Hyun Kyung, Korean theologian[1]

At some point back in the 1960s, many staunch churchgoers were shaken out of their insular comfort zone by the suggestion that before Holy Communion they might actually turn and greet the person in the pew next to them. The statement 'The peace of the Lord be always with you' was unknown in Church of England worship at that time, although the Peace wasn't quite a new invention of the Swinging Sixties. The practice of greeting with a 'holy kiss' (Romans 16.16, 1 Corinthians 16.20; 2 Corinthians 13.12) had been common among the first Christians, and 'the Peace' had remained in the Church until Reformation times.

Now it's customary for everyone to turn and use these words as a greeting to those around them. Usually there's an accompanying handshake, maybe even a hug. For some people this is still something of an awkward moment, and it's worth noting that there's no rule that you have to join in. But there are lots of reasons why it's a good thing to do, so let's explore a few of them.

People, not place

Maybe the reason for some people's discomfort, then and now, lies in that word 'churchgoer'. It implies an understanding that church is just a place or an event to be attended. But that is not what church is, or at least, not what Jesus intended. The Church, in its original meaning, is not a building but people.

'You are Peter,' said Jesus to his leading disciple, a man not known for his stability, 'and on this rock I will build my church' (Matthew 16.18).

We are being built together, says the Bible, 'into a dwelling-place for God' (Ephesians 2.22).

Can you be a Christian in isolation? Well, possibly, but it's not how things were intended to be. The two prime commandments in the Bible are to love God and love your neighbour and the two are inextricably linked.

So when we share the Peace together, what we're doing is acknowledging this connectedness. We're agreeing with the famous premise of seventeenth-century poet John Donne: 'No man is an island, entire of itself …'[2] and accepting that, while in one sense we come before God each one of us alone and individual, in another sense, we all come together.

It is also acknowledging that, whatever you might think of that person beside you, as far as God is concerned each of us is equally welcome. We come to the communion table as sinners and hypocrites all. God's offer of grace and peace is extended to you and to them in equal measure.

Inclusivity, not elitism

One would hope that this should never need to be spelt out – but church is not a secret society for the socially acceptable. Should, God forbid, you find yourself in a church like that, walk away with speed!

Church is for people of any background, all ethnic origins, all physical and mental abilities and disabilities, and especially for all ages. There is a lot to be said about inclusivity in church, and this book doesn't have the capacity to go into it, but just a brief word about children. Bringing children to church is of the most vital importance – for the children themselves, for families and not least, for the Church itself. It will die out if not!

But there is more to it than that. Jesus made a point of welcoming children (Luke 18.16), not just to show that he cared for them, but also to show the adults around how much they had to learn from them. Children are a vital part of what Jesus called 'the kingdom of heaven' and they bring something of the simple, joyous and uninhibited nature of that kingdom into church with them too.

Most churches cater for children in one way or another, either with Sunday morning children's groups or family services or a mixture of the two. But if as a parent you find yourself bringing your child to a service not particularly geared to children, please be reassured. Churches welcome children!

It can't be guaranteed that you will never encounter someone of the 'Children should be seen and not heard', 'It wasn't like this in my day' withering look variety, but if you do, don't let them get to you!

And children respond to worship. Of course, it's a delicate balance between allowing them enough freedom to feel at home and encouraging them, as they become old enough, to learn quietness and respect. But many children actually enjoy the atmosphere of music and stillness, of stained glass and candles and symbolism, without needing to understand it all. Children have a great capacity for wonder. (Again, something we could all learn from.)

So, if you bring children to church, feel free to talk to them quietly about what they are experiencing. Search out some children's Bible story books, or use the resources listed in the back of the book, which explain more about the communion service, and look at these together.

Of course, younger children won't have the attention span for an adult sermon, so do bring something with you to keep them amused (nothing noisy obviously). Some churches even provide 'quiet bags' with activities or books in them.

But to return to the focus of this chapter: the sharing of the Peace – it's a great opportunity to teach children that *everyone* is special and made in God's image. And a great opportunity as adults to remind ourselves as well. So if you find yourself near a child, make sure to greet them too.

Diversity, not discord

A little word here about that little word 'peace'. What the Bible means by it is not just tranquillity and absence of conflict. The old Hebrew word 'shalom' has a much broader meaning of well-being and wholeness.

Churches on the whole are not known for absence of conflict. Rare is the church where everyone is in agreement – and, if so, it's probably because all those who disagree have moved off to the church down the road! People tend to feel strongly about things – whether it's dismantling the pews, ordaining women, or allowing children to run up and down the aisle. And it's right that they should. Real 'shalom' does not mean avoiding confrontation, but dealing with difference wisely and respectfully. So, when you offer the 'peace' to someone, this too is what you are offering them – not a promise that you will never disagree, but that you will allow them the privilege of holding views other than your own. Who knows, God might actually agree with them!

Prayer, not politeness

So, when we share the Peace, it's a lot more than a burst of forced politeness, or an artificial show of affection. The words 'The peace of

THE PEACE

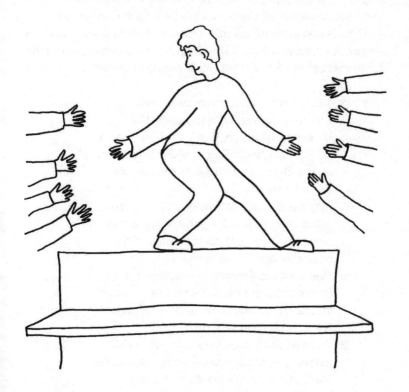

BEAR IN MIND THAT IT IS NOT A
COMPETITION TO SHAKE AS MANY
HANDS AS POSSIBLE

the Lord be with you' aren't just a religious version of 'Hi there', or 'Dahling' air-kissing. They are a prayer. As you greet someone, you are asking God to bring them wholeness and well-being, and they in return are asking for wholeness and well-being to come on you.

There is also more to this than greeting those you know and like already. It's a time to look beyond. And there are many additional things that can be said without words during this time:

- Maybe you need to make peace with someone, to offer an apology or rebuild a broken relationship. This is the ideal time to do it. In fact, according to Jesus, before you approach the altar is exactly the time you should do it (Matthew 5.23-24). Sometimes it may need to be explicit. Very often, though, just an offered hand, a genuine smile and straightforward eye contact will heal the wound or bridge the gap.

- Maybe now is the time to welcome a stranger. Even if you feel a bit of a newcomer yourself, you can still make someone else feel welcome. Ask a name. Offer your own.

- Some people's body language will signal that they don't want anyone to get too close. Maybe they are shy. Maybe they need to use this time to get right with God. Show by keeping your distance that you respect who and where they are.

- Maybe it is appropriate to dare a hug, even with someone you hardly know. For some people this may be the only physical contact with another human being that they get all week.

- Don't be afraid of an added word here or there either. It's an ideal time to offer appreciation or praise.
- Perhaps you can comfort someone who is hurting. Watch for signs of need. Don't be afraid to spend time just with one person if they need it.
- And don't be afraid of letting your own need show. All of us are vulnerable at one time or another and it's nothing to be ashamed of. It's our common humanity we're sharing here.

The 'Peace' can be only a symbol of something much deeper, and probably more time-consuming. But it stands as a reminder that, if you are really serious about reaching out to God, then you will find him most readily in the person next door.

CHAPTER

8

Receiving and renewing

THE NEED FOR STRENGTH, COMFORT AND DELIGHT

The proper effect of the Eucharist is the transformation of man into God.

Thomas Aquinas, thirteenth-century Italian theologian[1]

So our typical service has taken us through the need to confess and give thanks, the need to understand and believe, and the need to care for the world and make peace with our neighbour. And now we arrive at the heart of it all, for many the most precious act that worship has to offer – the Holy Communion.

For a newcomer, though, it's an act all too often shrouded in mystifying ritual and unfamiliar language.

Unpacking the terminology

The meaning at the heart of this act is both deep and simple. However, to approach it, you may first need to get beyond what seems like a small morass of terminology.

What is often referred to as Holy Communion (from a Latin

term meaning 'sharing in common') is also frequently known as the Eucharist (a Greek word meaning 'gratitude or giving of thanks'). It may also be known as 'the Lord's Supper', 'the Lord's Table' or 'the Breaking of Bread' – terms that go straight back to its origins in the last meal Jesus shared with his disciples before his death.

Whatever it is called, it is one of the Church's two main sacraments, the other being baptism. A sacrament is defined as 'a means of grace' and, to unpack that a little more, you need to understand the word 'grace' as it is used here – God's free and unconditional goodness and favour to every one of us exactly as we are.

So, at heart, this simple matter of 'grace' is what the Communion is all about. God loves you unconditionally; God wants you to be all you have the potential to be; God wants to give you good gifts.

But there's an old saying: 'God's grace is free, but it is not cheap.' Communion is a reminder that it was paid for at great cost.

Appreciating what's on offer

For theologians and others who study this sort of thing, the idea of grace is used in two ways. First, what's known as *common grace*: sunset, laughter, a field of poppies, a baby's smile – all the many delights of the natural world that surround us every day. But it's mainly the second idea of grace, sometimes called special grace, that Communion celebrates – that of God's gift of 'redemption'.

That's yet another idea that could take up a whole book to itself, but the basic idea can be found in the ordinary dictionary definition of the verb 'to redeem': 'to buy back, to recover or free by payment, to rescue, deliver, free, to reclaim, to pay the penalty of . . .'

Central to the Christian story is the idea that all humans are enslaved by 'sin' – back to another jargon word, but substitute 'selfishness and wrongdoing' and you'll get the idea. It goes something like this:

We know what we want to do and who we want to be, but all too often we're hooked by bad habits and wrong desires. These habits and desires lead us, at best, to be less than we could be, and at worst to become enmeshed in terrible errors that damage ourselves and others. This entrapment, says the Bible, leads inevitably to death – the death of the spirit as we become separated from God. We've lost our way and can't find the path back.

Perhaps there are a lucky few who can free themselves from their own mess by their own tenacity or wisdom. But most of us can't. We need help. This help, says the Bible, has come in one great act of redemption for all people, for all time.

The bread and wine of Communion sum this up. They are, in the words of the invitation spoken by the priest, from *Common Worship*:

> ...*the body of our Lord Jesus Christ*
> *which he gave for you,*
> *and his blood which he shed for you.*

God took human form in Jesus, took death on himself – the painful physical death of crucifixion and the deeper pain of spiritual death – and so paid the price for your wrongdoing so you don't have to. This is what redemption is all about.

Remembering the origins

Bread and wine as symbols of Jesus' body and blood are not interpretations dreamed up in retrospect after his death. They're rooted in something Jesus himself said to his puzzled disciples as they sat down for the meal known as the Last Supper:

> *While they were eating, Jesus took a loaf of bread,*
> *and after blessing it he broke it, gave it to the*
> *disciples and said 'Take, eat; this is my body.' Then*

> *he took a cup, and after giving thanks he gave it*
> *to them, saying, 'Drink from it, all of you; for this is*
> *my blood of the covenant, which is poured out for*
> *many for the forgiveness of sins.'*

Matthew 26.26-28

It was, in fact, no ordinary meal they were sharing, but one that was a central part of Jewish ritual – the Passover. So the roots go back even deeper, to the Old Testament story of the Hebrews' escape from slavery in Egypt.

Sacrifice as a means to appease the gods or effect change seems to be a primal instinct, practised by many ancient tribes, the Hebrews among them. On that night of escape, the old story goes, God told them to kill a lamb, cook it and daub the blood on their doorposts so that the angel of death would pass over them and destroy only the Egyptians with plague. This was to be the final sign that would convince the Pharaoh to release them.

So we can see many deep themes stretching back thousands of years – sacrifice, rescue, release – and there's one more, summed up in that little word 'covenant' that Jesus used in the quote above. It's the idea of a two-way promise between God and his people. If they for their part continued to trust and obey his commands, then God for his part would continue to bless them and give them freedom and dignity.

Of course, although the Hebrews (later known as the Jews) had been given the promise and responsibility of being God's chosen people, they often didn't remember their part of the bargain, and over the years it led them as a nation into decline, captivity or oppression. That's why this idea of remembering had become so important to them. The unleavened bread (a reminder of bread cooked hastily with no time to rise, ready for the Exodus journey) and the cups of wine (a reminder of the vineyards of the promised land they yearned for) told a story they needed to recall.

Likewise the Lord's Table tells a story we cannot afford to forget.

Exploring the symbols

Those are just some of the layers of meaning contained in the bread and wine. But they're not all. Bread and wine have a much more straightforward and maybe more profound symbolism, not just as part of the Christian or Jewish story, but simply as part of what it means to be human. We all need to eat and drink.

In our wealthy Western society, bread is just a small part of our diet, but throughout history and in most parts of the world today it is the staple of life. 'Give us this day our daily bread' is a heartfelt cry and not something that can be assumed.

We need nourishment. We need something to give us strength to get through the week and we need it not just physically, but spiritually as well. Jesus understood this and made an astonishing claim:

> I am the bread of life. Whoever comes to me will
> never be hungry, and whoever believes in me will
> never be thirsty.

John 6.35

Whatever our spiritual hunger – for love, acceptance, meaning, purpose – God through Jesus promises to satisfy it.

On another occasion Jesus also promised that 'those who drink of the water that I will give them will never be thirsty' (John 4.14). For obvious reasons, he chose wine rather than water to use as the liquid symbol of his sacrifice, but the same idea is present. The wine promises that God will slake our spiritual thirst.

But wine speaks of more than that. It also symbolizes enjoyment, celebration, frivolity even. God doesn't just want to keep us going on the journey of life, he wants to give us delight as we travel.

So these simple elements tell us that in the long hard slog that is everyday living, God will not let us down. He will renew, refresh and replenish us.

Accepting the blessing

There's one more bit of jargon that can't be avoided, and it's the controversial one of 'transubstantiation' – an idea strong in traditional Roman Catholic belief that the bread and wine, when taken by believers, literally turn into the flesh and blood of Christ. In centuries past it led, not surprisingly, to a rumour that Christians were cannibals!

It's a debate that can quickly turn to absurdity, and one we're not going to get into here, for the simple reason that both extremes – that the Communion is *either* literal flesh and blood *or* nothing more than symbolism and remembrance – are likely to miss the point. God is *real*. God *really* wants to bless us. Everything in our world, soil to sky, east to west, is infused with God's Spirit. God can choose to give *real* grace and *real* blessing through any medium he chooses – bread or wafers, wine or grape juice, solemn priests or little children. So when someone comes to the Communion table genuinely wanting to accept grace from God, then God is genuinely going to give it.

But the point, expressed by one of the Communion prayers, is that the bread and wine 'may be to us the body and blood of Christ'. The grace given here is far more than just the 'common' sort. It is the redemptive sort, the sort that can come only from the sacrifice of Jesus. It really doesn't matter how it works. The point is – it does!

Understanding the etiquette

A word here is needed about the etiquette of a newcomer receiving communion.* The official Church of England line is that the sacrament of Communion should come only after the rites of baptism and confirmation, but baptized members of other mainstream churches

*If you are physically unable to come up to the altar rail, please alert one of the sidespeople as you come into church, and they will ensure that communion is brought down to you.

are welcome to take communion too. If you have not been confirmed, you may still come to the communion rail but keep your hands down rather than cupped to receive the bread and the priest will then pray a blessing over you. (If you're not sure what to do, maybe go for a blessing the first time and speak to the priest afterwards about what is appropriate for you.) The same is true for children who, unless they have been confirmed or been through an 'admission to communion' course, should come to the communion rail for a prayer of blessing. And again, for adults and children, God is quite capable of giving *real* grace and *real* blessing through this act too.

What all churches are agreed on is this: you don't need to understand every detail of the Christian faith in order to receive God's grace. You don't need to be a good person, a respectable person, a churchy person, a person who understands it all, or a person who thinks they've got everything sorted. In fact, if you think you are, you're probably coming in quite the wrong spirit. The prayer immediately before the Communion, often known as the Prayer of Humble Access, sums it all up:

> *We do not presume*
> *to come to this your table, merciful Lord,*
> *trusting in our own righteousness,*
> *but in your manifold and great mercies.*
> *We are not worthy*
> *so much as to gather up the crumbs under your table.*
> *But you are the same Lord*
> *whose nature is always to have mercy . . .*

Common Worship

As human beings we were made with needs, not just for food and drink, but for mercy and grace. Receiving them requires just two things: humility and trust. God will do the rest.

CHAPTER

Pilgrimage and participation

THE NEED TO SHARE
THE JOURNEY

We are pilgrims on a journey,
fellow-travellers on the road.
We are here to help each other
walk the mile and bear the load.

Richard Gillard, from 'The Servant Song'[1]

The communion is completed. The service is nearly at an end. Together priest and people ask God to 'Send us out . . . to live and work to your praise and glory' (*Common Worship*).

What has been happening in this hour or so is not just a peaceful interlude in a busy week. It is intended to be the very foundation of that week. You are being sent out to make a difference to your world. To bring, even into the very ordinary things you do each day, a tiny trace of God's glory. And you are not intended to leave empty handed. You are intended to go out 'in the power of the Holy Spirit' and with heart and mind kept stable by 'the peace of God which passes all understanding'. And this is vital to remember. You don't leave God behind you as you leave. God is with you in every part of your journey, with you equally in your mistakes and disappointments as in your joys and successes.

So as you prepare to leave, before the rest of life takes over, take a tiny moment of quiet to make this prayer your own. If what you do in church doesn't have an impact on your life outside, then you may as well stay home with the Sunday papers.

Coffee and conversation

At the end of the service the priest proclaims:

Go in peace to love and serve the Lord.

At which point you may have a choice – to scuttle off and resume normal life, or in many churches, to join others at the back or in the hall for tea, coffee and biscuits.

There's something valuable at times in going to church anonymously. You've gone to meet God and God alone. If now is a time when you need that kind of solitude, then that's fine.

But in the long term, it's not really what church was intended to be. A church service can help you worship, but 'church' in the terms that Jesus intended is rather more than that. What he meant was a community of his followers gathering together, learning together, journeying in faith together.

After his death and resurrection, the first Christians instinctively pitched into this lifestyle with gusto. They met daily to learn or pray. They ate together in each other's homes, they shared their possessions. It was clearly a lifestyle that attracted others – their numbers grew by the day (Acts 2.44-47).

All that may seem a long way from small talk over the chocolate digestives. But any sort of human relationship begins with tiny first steps. So even though small talk with a load of strangers isn't always easy, maybe it's the first step towards understanding what *being* part of a church, rather than just *going* to it, really means.

COFFEE TIME

THINGS TO TALK
ABOUT IF YOU
ARE A BIT
STUCK FOR IDEAS

THE CHURCH GROUPS
YOU ARE PLANNING
TO ATTEND

THINGS YOU WILL
BE DOING DURING
THE WEEK

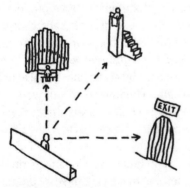

YOUR PEW/SEAT:
WHAT THE VIEW
WAS LIKE

YOUR PLANS
FOR LUNCH

Not that belonging to a church means some sort of mandatory first-believers-style all-in-togetherness. You no doubt have a busy life, and even if you could suddenly throw it all up to go to prayer meetings and Bible studies and run the toddler group, that might not be a great idea. God wants his people out there living authentic spiritual life in all parts of society, not tucked away in some holy huddle.

But if you are serious about living an authentic spiritual life, then you'll probably need some help and companionship as you set about it. So spending at least some time with others who are on the same quest as yourself is pretty much essential if you mean business.

And even if you're still not sure what you think about all this Christian stuff, getting a bit more involved is the best way to find out more about it.

It's also a great way to make some really good friends.

Availability and vulnerability

Services are just a small part of the life of most churches – spending time together informally and working together to serve others are seen as just as important. Many run house groups, Lent courses, discipleship classes, or Christian basics courses where you can discuss, share and learn in a relaxed small-group environment. They will probably have many other activities you could join: social action groups, choir, old people's lunch clubs, children's or youth work, for example. There's no better way to get to know others than to work alongside them – and there's also no better way to get to know a little more about yourself!

There's an old-fashioned word sometimes used in church circles – *fellowship*. It actually means something that can't quite be summed up any other way, something deeper than ordinary friendship. Indeed, it's something that can at times be shared with people you hardly know.

It's the sort of human relationship that begins when people have accepted Jesus' challenge to 'love one another as I have loved you' (John 15.12). It thrives among people who understand themselves to be 'sinners', among those who know themselves so loved by God that they don't have to prove anything to anyone else. It's a risky business this fellowship, demanding both vulnerability and availability. But if you find it, then you will have found what church is truly about.

Remarkably, even among the buttoned-up British, even among moderation-in-all-things Anglicans, even among people who sometimes bicker and whinge and struggle with small talk, such fellowship can be found. It's amazing what God can do with unpromising material. So think what he could do with you.

Going to church is fine. Being church is better.

Go in peace to love and serve the Lord.

Glossary

Every organization has its own jargon, not least the Church of England. Here are a few terms you might find it useful to know.

Advent – The four weeks leading up to Christmas, and the beginning of the Christian year. Traditionally a time to wait and prepare for celebrating Christ's birth, but also his second coming as foretold in the Bible.

Anglican – an adjective referring to those who are part of the Church of England or other churches of the *Anglican Communion* or who share its practices and beliefs.

Anglican Communion – an affiliation of churches worldwide, including Episcopalian churches in the USA, that share the same beliefs and practices as the Church of England. The Archbishop of Canterbury is one of the foci for unity of the entire Anglican Communion, but exercises legal authority only within the Church of England.

Baptism – the rite of entry into the Church, where an adult or a child is either sprinkled with or immersed in water. It is a symbol both of cleansing and of death and rising to new life, following the example of Jesus who was baptized at the beginning of his ministry. Often referred to as christening, although in fact the naming of the baby is not a formal part of the ritual.

Book of Common Prayer – the Church of England's first complete book of worship services in English, originally published in 1549. The definitive version of 1662 (sometimes simply referred to by that date) is still much loved for its beauty of language.

Catholic – The word literally means whole or inclusive and originally referred to the entire Church. Whilst the term 'Roman Catholic' refers to a completely separate church organization, the term 'catholic' used within the Church of England refers to the part of the church more concerned with tradition and ceremonial, sometimes also known as 'high' church.

Chalice – goblet containing the Communion wine.

Charismatic – a style of Christianity placing strong emphasis on the power and gifts of the Holy Spirit, and perhaps on lively and informal worship. It may be found in both the evangelical and catholic parts of the church.

Churchwardens – Two church members who act in a voluntary capacity as officials for the church. They are legally responsible for managing and maintaining the church property.

Collect – a prayer set for that particular Sunday intended to 'collect' together the prayers of the people.

Common Worship – the Church of England's current collection of worship services, mostly in contemporary language.

Confirmation – a ceremony at which a bishop 'lays hands on', in other words, blesses, a young person or adult who wishes to 'confirm' for themselves the baptismal vows made for them as a baby and commit themselves to following Christ. If the person was not previously baptized, then baptism and confirmation are often carried out together.

Curate – an assistant member of the clergy working either full- or part-time.

Diocese – a geographic area within the C of E, about the size of a county, but not necessarily relating to county boundaries, presided over by a diocesan bishop and containing a cathedral city.

Evangelical – sometimes also known as 'low church'. A style of churchmanship that places emphasis more on the Bible as Christian authority than on sacraments and church tradition. It may well be more informal in style, with less emphasis on ceremonial.

Eucharist – From the Greek for 'thanksgiving'. A service also known as 'Holy Communion' or the 'Lord's Supper' (see pp.53–9 for an explanation).

Evensong – a form of evening service, not including Holy Communion, often with most of the service sung by clergy and choir.

Genuflection – a mark of respect used in high churches, especially when someone moves out of the aisle to come forward for communion: a sort of deep curtsey, where the right knee goes down to the floor alongside the left foot. Sometimes replaced by a 'profound bow' – bowing from the waist rather than from the neck. Bowing often occurs at other points in the service, in particular when anyone enters the church or crosses in front of the altar.

Gradual hymn – the hymn before the Gospel reading, so called after the Latin word for step, because in medieval times the Gospel was always (and sometimes still is) taken up to the altar to be blessed before being read.

Lectionary – a book giving set Bible readings for each day of the year. There are usually an Old Testament reading, a New Testament reading and a Gospel reading. The lectionary used by most churches follows a three-year cycle.

Lent – a six-week period of the Christian year leading up to Easter. Traditionally a time of preparation for baptism or for the renewal of baptismal vows. Often used now as a time of self-denial, or of learning more about faith in Lent groups.

Liturgy – A set order of service including prayers and words spoken by minister and people.

Matins – the old Latin name for Morning Prayer, an order of service that does not include Holy Communion.

NSM (Non-Stipendiary Minister) – an ordained priest working in a voluntary capacity.

PCC (Parochial Church Council) – the executive council of a parish church, made up of clergy, churchwardens and members elected by the congregation.

Reader – someone not ordained as a priest but trained and licensed by the Church of England to preach and lead some services.

Sacrament – A ceremony of the Church through which, Christians believe, God acts in a particular significant way in blessing those who enter into it. The two main sacraments of the Anglican Church are baptism and Holy Communion.

Sign of the cross – Often used in 'higher' churches, most often at the Gospel reading, at the beginning of the Communion, and at the final blessing, when the words 'In the name of the Father, Son and Holy Spirit' are used. Using the right hand, the movement goes from forehead ('Father'), chest ('Son') and shoulders left to right ('Holy Spirit').

Thurible – A container for incense, sometimes swung at different times of the service. The incense symbolizes holiness and the worship of the people rising up as something sweet and pleasing to God.

Further reading

Useful resources

www.e-mmaus.org.uk Emmaus is a Christian basics and ongoing discipleship course from a broad church tradition.

uk.alpha.org Alpha is a study series on the basics of Christianity from an evangelical perspective. There are ten weekly evening sessions plus one day or weekend away. The website can tell you of a course near you.

www.biblereadingnotes.org.uk and **www.cwr.org.uk** offer a selection of daily Bible reading notes to buy.

www.cofe.anglican.org is the official Church of England web site, offering church news, some of the services of the church to download and a helpful section on prayer.

www.rejesus.co.uk has a variety of creative material about Jesus, his followers, spirituality, prayers, etc.

www.wordlive.org Daily Bible readings and notes online.

www.wordontheweb.co.uk offers daily Bible readings with comments and a prayer online.

Bible versions: some personal recommendations

For accessibility

Good News Bible (second edition 1994) – easy to read, probably the best introduction for a new reader.

For beauty of language

Authorized (King James) Version (1611) – the old and well-loved language, but not easy to understand for beginners and without the accuracy of more modern versions.

For accuracy

New International Version (1978). A good balanced compromise between the three needs of accuracy, fluency and accessibility.

New Revised Standard Version (1995). A new translation based on the King James version, with more contemporary and inclusive language.

Helpful books

On the Bible

David and Pat Alexander, *The Lion Handbook to the Bible*, Lion, 2002.

Michael Hinton, *The 100-minute Bible*, 100-minute Press, 2005. A quick read-at-a-sitting introduction to the main themes of the Bible.

On the basics of Christianity

Stephen Cottrell, Steven Croft, *Travelling Well*, Church House Publishing, 2000. Ideal for those just setting out on their journey of faith and for those who feel they may have lost their way, this book gives help and instruction in major areas of Christian life.

Jeffrey John, Rosemary Gallagher, John Trenchard, *This is our Faith*, Redemptorist, 1995. Popular presentation of church teaching, beautifully presented and illustrated, from a high church perspective but with broad appeal.

Tom Wright, *Simply Christian*, SPCK, 2006. Rooted in solid scholarship, but written in a lively and accessible style, this book describes the relevance of Christianity to the contemporary world. Tom Wright is the current Bishop of Durham and a world-renowned theologian.

On worship

Paul Bradshaw and Peter Moger (eds), *Worship Changes Lives: How it works, why it matters*, Church House Publishing, 2008. A full-colour booklet from the Church of England exploring what worship is and why it matters. Supporting material at www.transformingworship.org.uk.

Introducing children to worship

John Muir and Betty Pedley, *Come and Join the Celebration*, Church House Publishing, 2001. Resource book to help adults and children experience Holy Communion together.

Diana Murrie, *My Communion Book*, Church House Publishing, 2002. Designed for children to use alongside the adult communion service.

Diana Murrie and Margaret Withers, *The Communion Cube*, Church House Publishing, 2002. Illustrated cube for children to open up as a hands-on way of exploring what Communion is all about. Also *The Lord's Prayer Cube*.

On suffering

James Jones, *Why do People Suffer?*, Lion, 2007. Highly readable and well-illustrated introduction to the subject with bite-sized chapters and lots of quotes.

Harold S. Kushner, *When Bad Things Happen to Good People*, Avon, 1988. Best-seller written by a Jewish rabbi.

On prayer

Stephen Cottrell, *Praying Through Life*, Church House Publishing, 1998. Accessible guide on how to start, renew and expand your prayer life.

Philip Yancey, *Prayer – does it make any difference?*, Hodder & Stoughton, 2006. A personal quest to unravel the mysteries of prayer: lamenting the unexplainable and rejoicing in evidence from moving true stories from around the world.

On the Church

Stephen Tomkins, *A Short History of Christianity*, Lion, 2005. Good introductory guide to church history.

Notes and references

All Bible quotations are from the New Revised Standard Version unless otherwise stated.

Preface
1 *Common Worship* texts used in this book are taken from *Common Worship: Services and Prayers for the Church of England*, Church House Publishing, 2000.

A prayer at the start of worship
1 Karl Barth, *Fifty Prayers*, Westminster John Knox Press, 1985 (trans. David C. Stassen, 2005).

Chapter 1 What *are* you doing here?
1 Augustine of Hippo, from H. Ward and J. Wild (eds), *The Lion Christian Quotation Collection*, Lion, 1997.
2 *Good News Bible: Today's English Version* (British usage edn), The Bible Societies/Collins/Fontana, 1976.

Chapter 2 Wonder and wow factor
1 Dag Hammarskjold (trans. W. H. Auden and L. Sjoberg), *Markings*, Alfred A. Knopf, 1964.
2 Barry Schwartz, *The Paradox of Choice*, HarperCollins, 2004, p. 179.
3 Schwartz, 2004.

Chapter 3 Admitting and acknowledging
1 Jean Vanier, *Community and Growth*, Darton, Longman & Todd, 1979.
2 T. Castle (ed.), *The Hodder Book of Christian Quotations*, Hodder & Stoughton, 1982.
3 H. Ward and J. Wild (eds), *The Lion Christian Quotation Collection*, Lion, 1997.

Chapter 4 The Bible – and bashing it!
1 Samuel Taylor Coleridge in H. Ward and J. Wild (eds), *The Lion Christian Quotation Collection*, Lion, 1997.
2 *The New International Version* of the Bible is published by the International Bible Society, and is also available for Bible searches at www.biblegateway.com.
3 John Bunyan, *Grace Abounding to the Chief of Sinners*, 1666.

4 In T. Castle (ed.), *The Hodder Book of Christian Quotations*, Hodder & Stoughton, 1982.

5 From R. Backhouse (ed.), *The Ultimate Speakers' Handbook*, Zondervan, 1997.

6 Origin unknown – variously attributed to G. K. Chesterton, Garrison Keillor and Reinhold Niebuhr.

7 Harvey Cox, quoted in H. Ward and J. Wild (eds), *The Lion Christian Quotation Collection*, Lion, 1997.

Chapter 5 Bottom line or benchmark

1 T. S. Eliot in H. Ward and J. Wild (eds), *The Lion Christian Quotation Collection*, Lion, 1997.

2 Richard Dawkins, 'A Scientist's Case Against God', excerpt from a speech at Edinburgh International Science Festival in *The Independent*, 20 April 1992.

3 Lewis Carroll, *Through the Looking Glass: and what Alice found there* – many editions available.

Chapter 6 Problems and petitions

1 M. Gandhi, *Non-violence in Peace and War*, Navajivan Publishing House, 1942.

2 Douglas V. Steere, quoted in H. Ward and J. Wild (eds), *The Lion Christian Quotation Collection*, Lion, 1997.

3 Louis Bouyer, quoted in H. Ward and J. Wild (eds), *The Lion Christian Quotation Collection*, Lion, 1997.

4 Much reworded phrase originally based on paper by Edward Lorenz, 'Does the flap of a butterfly's wings in Brazil set off a tornado in Texas?' 1972, quoted in Z. Sadar and I. Abrams (eds), *Chaos for Beginners*, Icon, 1998.

5 Catherine Bramwell-Booth, quoted in M. Batchelor, *Catherine Bramwell-Booth*, Lion, 1986.

6 C. S. Lewis, *The World's Last Night*, Harcourt Brace Jovanovich, 1973.

Chapter 7 Handshakes and hugs

1 Chung Hyun Kyung from H. Ward and J. Wild (eds), *The Lion Christian Quotation Collection*, Lion, 1997.

2 John Donne, *Devotions upon Emergent Occasions*, 'Meditation 17', 1624.

Chapter 8 Receiving and renewing

1 Thomas Aquinas, from H. Ward and J. Wild (eds), *The Lion Christian Quotation Collection*, Lion, 1997.

Chapter 9 Pilgrimage and participation

1 From Richard Gillard, 'The Servant Song', © 1977 Scripture in Song/Maranatha Music, administered by Copy Care (music@copycare.com). Used by permission.